I am handing over to you now.

*Go find your way and come back
to tell me what I haven't even
dreamed of yet.*

From *The Intuitive Writing Craft* seminar
by Joseph Williams

RISING

by
Najiba Mrakadeh

Contents

Gliding *1*
Sinking *2*
Bleeding *6*
Enduring *7*
Grieving *8*
Rising *9*
Her *13*
He saw the light* *14*
Breathing *16*
Setting seed *18*
Sacrament *19*
Serenity *21*
Let's *22*
If only I could love once more *23*
The ways to know *24*
And the window *26*
Acknowledgement *30*

Gliding

The light glints on the grey horizon.
Trees dazzle through the mist.
A mosaic of small villages
breathing.
I rise.

Sinking

Hard to hold onto life.
Hard to keep the laugh from bouncing away to dust.
Hard not to let the bleeding reach the gutter.
Hard to bounce hope up and down and keep hold.

This breath feels like the last, grips the cavity wall
of now
with its mucky hints of failure,
the oasis illusion,
its lying eyes and the dry throat
of a loner standing in a crowd.

A face appears. A flickering of life stirs.
Then the face turns to go and leaves
a hole in the tender earth of the heart

It is hard getting up to welcome a new day
with the day before still sitting on your chest,
its dark varnish still on your soul.

What's left of laughter?
Its bubble bursts in palms that hold the strength
of a gladiator lying dead.

Waiting.
Still waiting,
for a phone to ring,
for the doorbell to ring,
for a hand to open the curtains,
for a smile to call you in,
for a bed warmed by the heat of the other person,
for a kiss to call life out of your cells,
for a flow of energy soldiers to pull you up,
to lift you up,
to get you up
before your bed becomes a sea of fire.

But you know,
you are lying in no house and no bed.
You are lying in an open space
under the sky's star-pierced umbrella.

You are still perhaps waiting
for the sun to rise at midnight.
A sun for you, for you only.
Because you are worth all the bother,
the attention and the love.

Slipping away is such a delicious thought.

It slides as a serpent slides into the bushes.
It slips into your backyard,
then into your foundations.
It caresses you to sleep.
It holds you much tighter
than the mother's grip on her drowning child.
It touches you more kindly than a lover's kiss.
It pleasures you for an intense second of ecstasy,
collapsing into warm fatigue,
no effort, no pain, no bother.

Why stay then . . . ?
You are not you.
They are strangers, those ghosts.
And home is only stones and brittle mortar.
It is freezing when you are cold.

It is hell when you are hot.
And there is no right time,
no right place,
nor right earth.

As I crossed the road to post the letter,
She, not a lover, not a friend and not a neighbour, said:
"don't call it depression, describe it,
call it lack of energy, feeling a bit low today."
Her voice disrupted my thoughts
of looking for an instant cure for bleeding pain,
a violent blow, a speeding car.

I saved myself then,
but I sink today, sliding into a hole.
I take a deep breath and close my eyes.
Not knowing if I will hold on to the light
or slide into the unknown.

Bleeding

We bleed most for the sins we haven't committed,
for the fire of wanting still unseen,
for the shivering of longing never felt,
for the forbidden fruit we have not even planted.

Enduring

They travelled for so long.
They came so far.
Their journey into dark,
into earth,
into air.
They savoured the mud.
Sucked leaves for the milk of dew,
Ground stones for hope.

They, she, he, or it explode into many colours,
Gender,
Shape,
Aroma,
Liquid,
Solid.

Grieving

I climbed the mountain peak to catch the light beams
and swing for a treat,
and see beyond my grief.

I sunk deep in the ocean, to catch its thread
and knit a tomorrow,
but the waves spat me out.

I fell clawing the earth,
waiting … for a new tomorrow.

Rising

Injection in, the dye spreads,
traces the flow of blood.
The trolley moves slowly into darkness.
Pulse races,
veins bubble with light,
layer after layer falls and melts.
The veins open as specks of gold, race like a serpent,
into the pitch black
to capture, to scrawl,
inscribe, enfold.
A flash of gold strikes inwards,
to where freedom lies
a stretched ruin to infinity,
a single gleam of light.

The barking wind wakes her shuttered eyes,
The brushing Autumn leaves open her cells. They breathe.
Shivers run through her.
She lifts her hand as far as the shaking will permit
and smells the sickening iron spice

of the chains that hold her breath.
Dust of years, sweat of centuries
is the glue that secures her stillness.

A hymn awakens in her throat,
a drop of time in one ear,
and light and water stream into her.
Her cells start to blossom like
roses
trading rapture for skin soaked in blood.

They, who are devoted to her,
coming out of an angry earth, seeking light,
surging up from an erupting volcano,
their bodies burned with life,

Moving a mountain with their tiny hands,
blowing back the storm with their short breath,
carrying bodies full of bullet holes
with their light and their water, they caress her.
They wash her eyes with their tears,
and touch her with the light of
their seeing.

Their feet have melted into earth.
Their bodies carry wounds like olive trees.
Their eyes bear souls in the retina.

They share their lungs as the dust fills them.
The night rewards them with a moon
to see their ghostly shapes, their shining souls,
then sacks the moon
as they cry blood and infertile seeds.
Their wailing brings night to its knees,
reaches the skies and tears down their curtains,
begging for a holy voice to put them to sleep.

A tear wells up in the earth's eyes
and falls to freedom's lips.
She smiles.

She ….
her eyes of zephyr,
her nose, flowers pollen,
her cheeks, dark red damask rose petals,
her hair, a thousand fountains of night strings,

her fingers, tender growth of trees,
her perfume, the breeze of waves.

A hymn awakens in her throat.
She smiles, her bearing is for more.

Is it late or early? How will she know?

Her

Her?
She was sung in a poem.
Chanted in the quiet of souls.
A woman who bears pain to bear life.
Is she the creation of suffering,
the hallucination of a dying voice?

Water her.
Dream for her.
Seek her in every pulse.
Fresh wind surging
like a flight of arrows,
her body dissolving into earth.

She holds back the volcano's eruption,
the vast flood of carelessness,
the wild storm of blindness,
holds them all to release them
for an ecstasy shorter than the blink of an eye

that ripples forever as hope.

He saw the light*

"In my end is my beginning." T.S. Eliot, "Four Quartets" Part II: East Coker

He smiled when he saw light among the rubble that blocked the way.
He saw tomorrow when hell and fire descended.
We in the crowd of bodies smelt fear, smelt death.
He saw light among the rubble that blocked the way.

"Why bother?" voices asked.
"Lie down, make a hole, crawl, until you get a chance to live."
Neither death nor promises of wealth could hold him back.

"In my end is my beginning."

He stood for the hope of future embryos.
He saw tomorrow when hell and fire descended.
He saw light among the rubble that blocked the way.

* Bassel Shehadeh (January 31, 1984 – May 28, 2012) was a Syrian Christian film-maker, producer, IT Engineer, environmental and cultural activist, and a well-known civil activist during the civil war from 2011 to 2012. He was a pioneer in organising peaceful protests in Damascus denouncing the government's crackdown of the Arab Spring. His camera captured and documented the assaults and bombardments conducted by the Syrian regime's forces on the city of Homs. He was killed during a government assault in the neighbourhood of al-Safsafa in Homs.

Breathing

We step out of place, out of time, and reach in.

I fly to the tree and hold tight the soft branch.
The breeze plays, racing through the leaves.

Breathe

The first breath is short, too low.
I shiver.
The branch under my claws shivers too.

Waves run through the leaves.

Breathe

As the sun slips through,

Breathe

I smile, drunk, and fall,
landing on elastic earth.

I Breathe

My body reaches out for more,
the earth reaches out to keep hold of me.

I have eyes.
I open them
to a stained blue spot of light,
brushed by the blue of my eyes.

Setting seed

I close my eyes and hear the whisper of the leaves,
the laughter of the grass,
the hissing of an ancient tree.
I hear the cry of a hanged body,
calling from dry lips and deserted veins.

I feel a kiss on my cheek,
a feather touching my skin.

I cry a foam of thirst.
I float into the trees.
I sink into the earth.
I melt into a thousand seeds.

Sacrament

I arrived there, why?
I don't remember, I don't know.
I was in the middle of it,
the human voices were rising,
the plates and the cutlery clicking and banging.
The wind was howling, the trees were weeping and the
light was shaking.

I stood in the heart of their storm,
their glasses were raised, their arms stretched to the sky.
Cheers to me, they chanted.
I sank into deafness,
became a gentle cat or a soft toy.

This is how they invited me to their world,
a saviour, a replacement,
an umbrella for their anger and their pain.

Their world seemed fascinating
but it was cold and frightening.
I was caught in their eyes,
a butterfly in a wet spring
fixed in a cage to be displayed, admired.
I blinded my sight to free my wings
when I reached beyond the crystal ball.

The fresh air's knife cut me in two,
the bright sun burned me into ashes,
the breeze speared me,
a bitter sweet feed for the bees.

I came not knowing why.
I stayed not knowing how.
I vanished into a photo
on a fireplace.

Serenity

Not what I thought it would be. A long, narrow corridor barely lit; colourless paint harmful for the eyes. Curved walls dipped in the ocean then left with dry salt to decorate the window, a room sunk in the sand of the Sahara with air that's full of dust.

Deaf sounds muttering. No meaning to understand.

A room like the space between the cells of a brain, expanding as a tumour to accommodate the nothingness. A bed but no sleep. It is a bargain to be comfortable, swapping sanity for an ideal home, a tiny cell in the corner of my palm.

Let's . . .

Let's dance over a rope,
Love the comfort of our skeletons.
Let's travel further than our dreams.
Let's sing the chords that have rusted in our throats,
and the melody that's still in the cells of our brain.

Let's talk,
in each other's presence if you can bear it,
in silence if facing it makes you cry.

Let's kiss,
from a distance,
from the corner of your face
where it hurts but it's worth the pain.

Let's leave,
our death coats float in shrinking dreams
where joy hangs in a spider's web,
and the sunlight's caught in a drop of rain.

If only I could love once more

If only I could love once more,
I could baptise you with a waterfall of tears,
of dew, of a newborn baby's breath.

If only I could love once more,
I would climb that bridge,
and leap into the river with such strength,
printing my soul on its tiny stones.

If only I could love once more,
I would whisper into the air,
then listen to the trembling of leaves,
glowing like spring in the heart of a volcano.

The ways to know

We went on a hunt,
my sisters and I.

I went to find the moon,
Lama went to find the sun,
Maha to find the ways.

Our journeys were long.

I found the moon.
It is round like the khubz we eat,
it is bright like mum's kisses,
and changes too, to a crescent,
like dad's promises.

Lama found the sun.
It hides above the clouds that shadow us,
it could burn your skin,
like porridge left too long on the stove.

Maha searched for the ways,
she found too many,
too little time,
too many choices.
We came back with the sun, with the moon,
and a heavy bag of ways.

I hung the moon on the night.
Lama hung the sun on the day,
and Maha, poor Maha,
she has not been back for supper,
she walks around the universe,
scattering the ways, ways to journey,
ways to know.

And the window . . .

Through a forest not far from the top of the mountain, between the trunks of its trees hides a lake, barely visible, and an ornate town shines like a star in the barren night. Behind, through the ascending branches, a dark green mountain watches.

The morning mist peels off its sheet from the blue sky in all its shades. The trees glow. The rain falls like a secret, and its drops moan when the grass touches them in play. In this sacred place, in absolute silence, a music plays that does not stop for creatures or for the inanimate.

It had been a day soaked in light and splendour and now evening was approaching. A storm was brewing on the mountaintop.

An old wooden house rested in the heart of this forest, hidden out of sight of all the universe, except the trees that danced on a rainy night and the ants marching past the door. On that evening, the door opened, and two women came out, one in her seventies, let's call her Hope, and the other in her sixties, we'll call her Light.

Hope said: "do you hear?"
Light said: "do you see?"
Then they sat in silence.
The storm by now had arrived. The trees shook with fear. The mad dance began, and church bells rang in clamouring harmony as the clouds crossed the summits of the mountains.

The wise lady and her friend sat in silence. They drank toast after toast till the storm had traversed the hills.

The trees took a deep breath and came to rest, the birds sang again. In the last of the wind a tall tree swayed, its branches flexed like the fingers of a young pianist. An older tree bowed her head towards them in tenderness then returned to stability. This was what Light saw. The pulse of the forest is what Hope heard. She listened as her friend watched.

As the day started to gather itself up and depart, they went back inside the wooden house and closed the door.

Hope said: "leave one window open - we need some air when we light the stove."

Then they drank a toast to their friendship. Their stories began to come out of their shells. Hope spoke about her trees, her mountains, and the white peaks. Light spoke of the places in her mind she had touched on.

Their stories flew, and sleep flew from their eyes, and they danced in the fields of their youth until tears lulled them into bed. Their deep sleep renewed them as the seasons renew the year. All the while the window stood a little open, listening.

The light glints on the
grey horizon.

I rise.

Acknowledgement

The book cover: Image Lake 03. © Hugh Burden
www.hughburdenart.co.uk

The intuitive writing craft seminar by Joseph Williams brought my work into the light.
www.intuitivewritingcraft.com

Layout and typesetting by Anthony Lane
anthonylane13@protonmail.com

Special thanks to:

Belinda Rimmer

Cathryn Mahoney

Colette Campbell

Heather Nadir-Jones

Lizzie Leigh

Samantha Cooke

www.najibamracadeh.com

Milton Keynes UK
Ingram Content Group UK Ltd.
UKHW041944121123
432434UK00003B/46